IMMIGRANTS

IMMIGRANTS

A LIBRARY OF CONGRESS BOOK

BY MARTIN W. SANDLER

Introduction by James H. Billington, Librarian of Congress

HarperCollins*Publishers*

For Louis Sage, who lived the immigrant experience and realized the immigrant's dream

The author wishes to thank Robert Dierker, former senior advisor for multimedia activities of the Library of Congress and Dana Pratt, former director of publishing of the Library of Congress, for their encouragement and cooperation. Appreciation is expressed to Kate Murphy, Carol Weiss, Heather Henson, Liza Baker, Alan Bisbort, the staff of the Prints and Photographs Division of the Library of Congress, Dennis Magnu of the Library's Photoduplication Service and Judith Gray of the American Folklife Center. As with all the books in this series, this volume and its author owe much to the editorial skill and guidance of Kate Morgan Jackson.

◆

Immigrants
A Library of Congress Book

Library of Congress Cataloging-in-Publication Data
Sandler, Martin W.
Immigrants / by Martin W. Sandler ; introduction by James H. Billington.
p.   cm.
"A Library of Congress book."
ISBN 0-06-024507-7. — ISBN 0-06-024508-5 (lib. bdg.)
1. Immigrants—United States—History—Juvenile literature.   2. United States—Emigration and immigration—History—Juvenile literature.
3. Immigrants—United States—Pictorial works—Juvenile literature.   4. United States—Emigration and immigration—Pictorial works—Juvenile literature.
I. Title.
JV6450.S25   1995   93-44126
304.8'73—dc20   CIP
                                                                                                                                                              AC

Design by Tom Starace with Jennifer Goldman
1   2   3   4   5   6   7   8   9   10
❖
First Edition

Our type of democracy has depended upon and grown with knowledge gained through books and all the other various records of human memory and imagination. By their very nature, these records foster freedom and dignity. Historically they have been the companions of a responsible, democratic citizenry. They provide keys to the dynamism of our past and perhaps to our national competitiveness in the future. They link the record of yesterday with the possibilities of tomorrow.

One of our main purposes at the Library of Congress is to make the riches of the Library even more available to even wider circles of our multiethnic society. Thus we are proud to lend our name and resources to this series of children's books. We share Martin W. Sandler's goal of enriching our greatest natural resource—the minds and imaginations of our young people.

The scope and variety of Library of Congress print and visual materials contained in these books demonstrate that libraries are the starting places for the adventure of learning that can go on whatever one's vocation and location in life. They demonstrate that reading is an adventure like the one that is discovery itself. Being an American is not a patent of privilege but an invitation to adventure. We must go on discovering America.

James H. Billington
The Librarian of Congress

The American experience is filled with stories of men and women who in every era have faced enormous challenges and overcome them. None of these stories is more inspiring than that of the millions of people who, particularly between 1870 and 1920, crossed a wild and dangerous ocean in search of freedom and opportunity in a new land. It is an extraordinarily important story as well. For so much of who we are, what we are and what we have accomplished as a nation is due in the largest measure to the sacrifices made and the achievements realized by those who bore the name *immigrants*.

MARTIN W. SANDLER

LEAVING FOR A NEW WORLD

In the last quarter of the 1800's the United States is about to change dramatically. As the Statue of Liberty stands guard on its eastern shore, millions of newcomers pour into America.

These newcomers are called immigrants. Most come from countries throughout Europe. They are willing to risk everything for the chance to build new lives in what they have heard is a golden land.

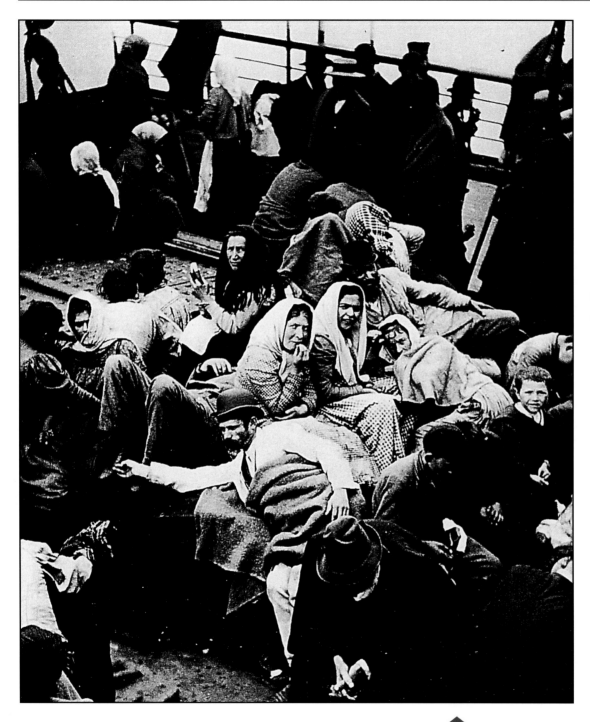

Their travels have taken them thousands of miles across a wild and dangerous ocean. The ocean voyage is only the first of many challenges they will face.

M ost will settle in the teeming American cities. Others will begin their new lives in the vast lands of the American West. Those who do not speak English will have to learn a new language. All will have to adapt to new ways of life.

The immigrants' children are at the center of their dreams. They are the hope for the future. Because of them, their parents are willing to face the unknown.

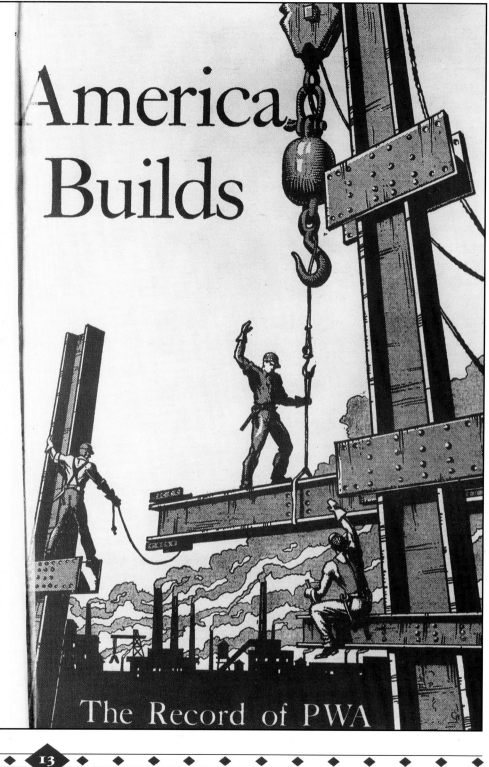

America Builds

The Record of PWA

The sacrifices will be great, but the immigrants will make them. They will have no choice but to work long hours at jobs others are unwilling to undertake. They will see that their children are educated in the ways of a new world. They will transform the nation and help build a new America.

THE LONG JOURNEY

The millions of men, women and children who will pour into America are both pulled and pushed into the New World. They are pulled by false stories of the quick riches and easy life they will find in the United States. They are pushed out of the Old World by harsh conditions that include hunger, poverty and religious and political persecution. Many of the families are so poor they are evicted from their homes.

Immigration to the United States by Country of Origin: 1820–1925   Total: 36,307,892

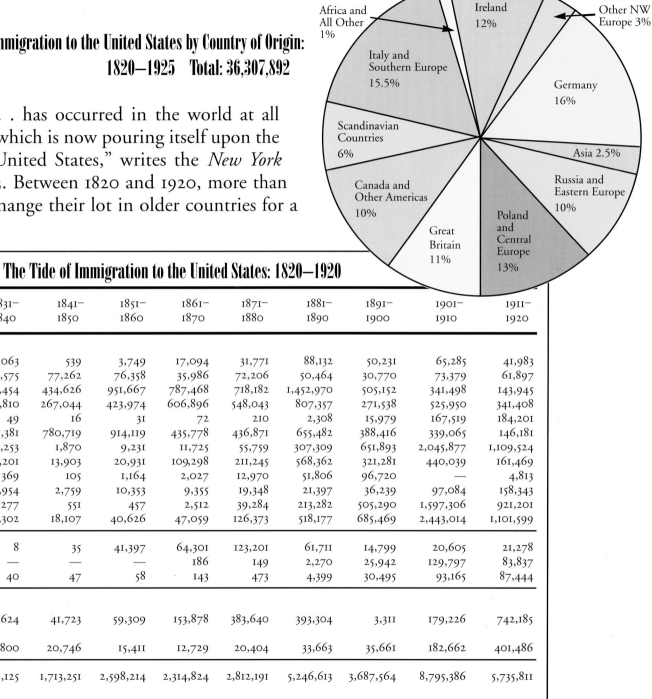

"No migration . . . has occurred in the world at all similar to that which is now pouring itself upon the shores of the United States," writes the *New York Tribune* in 1873. Between 1820 and 1920, more than 30 million people will exchange their lot in older countries for a new life in America.

The Tide of Immigration to the United States: 1820–1920

Country	1820–1830	1831–1840	1841–1850	1851–1860	1861–1870	1871–1880	1881–1890	1891–1900	1901–1910	1911–1920
Denmark	189	1,063	539	3,749	17,094	31,771	88,132	50,231	65,285	41,983
France	8,868	45,575	77,262	76,358	35,986	72,206	50,464	30,770	73,379	61,897
Germany	7,729	152,454	434,626	951,667	787,468	718,182	1,452,970	505,152	341,498	143,945
United Kingdom	27,489	75,810	267,044	423,974	606,896	548,043	807,357	271,538	525,950	341,408
Greece	20	49	16	31	72	210	2,308	15,979	167,519	184,201
Ireland	54,338	207,381	780,719	914,119	435,778	436,871	655,482	388,416	339,065	146,181
Italy	439	2,253	1,870	9,231	11,725	55,759	307,309	651,893	2,045,877	1,109,524
Norway/Sweden	94	1,201	13,903	20,931	109,298	211,245	568,362	321,281	440,039	161,469
Poland	21	369	105	1,164	2,027	12,970	51,806	96,720	—	4,813
Spain/Portugal	2,796	2,954	2,759	10,353	9,355	19,348	21,397	36,239	97,084	158,343
Russia (U.S.S.R.)	89	277	551	457	2,512	39,284	213,282	505,290	1,597,306	921,201
Other Europe	4,436	6,302	18,107	40,626	47,059	126,373	518,177	685,469	2,443,014	1,101,599
China	3	8	35	41,397	64,301	123,201	61,711	14,799	20,605	21,278
Japan	—	—	—	—	186	149	2,270	25,942	129,797	83,837
Other Asia	12	40	47	58	143	473	4,399	30,495	93,165	87,444
Canada and Newfoundland	2,486	13,624	41,723	59,309	153,878	383,640	393,304	3,311	179,226	742,185
Central and South America	9,465	19,800	20,746	15,411	12,729	20,404	33,663	35,661	182,662	401,486
All Countries	151,824	599,125	1,713,251	2,598,214	2,314,824	2,812,191	5,246,613	3,687,564	8,795,386	5,735,811

By 1890, New York City alone will have twice as many Irish as Dublin, half as many Italians as Naples, as many Germans as Hamburg and two and a half times as many Jewish people as Warsaw. Harsh as conditions at home may be, it is not an easy decision to leave one's homeland and friends and relatives. It is an emotional and difficult experience, but in villages, towns and cities throughout Europe, scenes of sad farewell become commonplace.

Farewell to old Ireland,
*   the land of my childhood,*
Which now and forever I am
*   going to leave. . .*
I'm bound to cross o'er that
*   wide swelling ocean*
In search of fame, fortune and
*   sweet liberty.*
—From song,
"The Emigrant's Farewell"

Good-byes also take place in European ports that become dominated by ships and people leaving for America.

I can remember only the hustle and bustle of those last weeks in Pinsk, the farewells from the family, the embraces and the tears. Going to America then was almost like going to the moon.

—Golda Meir, Russian Jewish immigrant

Many immigrants had brought on board balls of yarn, leaving one end of the line with someone on land. As the ship slowly cleared the dock, the balls unwound amid the farewell shouts of the women, the fluttering of the handkerchiefs, and the infants held high. After the yarn ran out, the long strips remained airborne, sustained by the wind, long after those on land and those at sea had lost sight of each other.

—Luciano DeCrescenzo, "The Ball of Yarn"

The trip from their towns and villages to the port cities is just the first step on the immigrants' long journey. Ahead lies the long and often dangerous sea voyage to America. The trip can take from five weeks to six months. Passengers are packed tightly aboard the ship, with little room to move about.

Crossing the Atlantic is a miserable experience. The wooden ships pitch and roll in the high seas, and many passengers are seasick throughout the entire voyage. The threat of fire from a lighted candle or an open cooking fire is all too real. Disease spreads through many vessels, and there is the constant danger of the ships' being destroyed in a fierce ocean storm.

Oh God, I was sick. Everybody was sick. I don't ever want to remember anything about that old boat. One night I prayed to God that it would go down because the waves were washing over it. I was that sick, I didn't care if it went down or not. And everybody else was the same way.

—Bertha Devlin, Irish immigrant

Because they are poor, most of the immigrants are forced to make the journey in the least expensive section of the ship, below the deck. Originally designed to transport animals and freight, this steerage section, as it is called, is a terribly crowded, filthy place with little air and little room to move about. Most steerage passengers endure almost the entire voyage without ever breathing fresh air or seeing the open sky.

Passengers on the vessels are not all poor. Thousands of wealthier men, women and children also seek a new and freer life in America. They can afford the higher fares that allow them to travel above deck, far removed from the steerage section.

As time passes, ocean travel does improve. By the 1870's, many sailing ships are replaced by steam-driven vessels. The journey is still dangerous, and life in the steerage section is still terribly difficult, but the speedier steamships reduce the ocean voyage to about fourteen days.

ARRIVING IN A NEW LAND

The voyage to America claims the lives of thousands of immigrants through disease or shipwreck, but the vast majority complete the difficult trip. More than 70 percent arrive in the great port of New York City. The millions who enter New York Harbor after 1886 are greeted by a sight they will never forget. It is the Statue of Liberty, symbol of the hopes and dreams of all who make the journey.

The Statue of Liberty is a gift from the people of France to the people of the United States. It is the creation of Frederic Auguste Bartholdi, whose dream was to build a monument honoring the American spirit of freedom that has inspired the world. In 1874, scores of skilled French laborers begin work on the statue.

The first time I saw the Statue of Liberty all the people were rushing to the side of the boat. "Look at her, look at her," and in all kind of tongues. "There she is, there she is," like it was somebody who was greeting them.

—Elizabeth Phillips, Irish immigrant

The Statue of Liberty is designed to stand 151 feet and one inch high from its base to the torch that Miss Liberty will hold in her hand. It will weigh 225 tons. Long before it is completed, news of the extraordinary gift causes great excitement in America. In 1876, the completed torch is shipped to the United States, where it becomes a major attraction at America's one hundredth birthday celebration in Philadelphia.

On May 21, 1884, more than twelve years of work on the Statue of Liberty are completed. The monument is dismantled and shipped to New York in 214 enormous packing crates. It is then reassembled and re-erected on Bedloe's Island in New York Harbor. On October 28, 1886, President Grover Cleveland leads the festivities as the statue is officially dedicated.

I felt grateful the Statue of Liberty was a woman. I felt she would understand a woman's heart.

—Stella Petrakis,
Greek immigrant

Give me your tired, your poor,
Your huddled masses yearning to breathe free,
The wretched refuse of your teeming shore.
Send these, the homeless, tempest-tossed to me,
I lift my lamp beside the golden door!

—From the poem "The New Colossus"
by Emma Lazarus, inscribed on the
pedestal of the Statue of Liberty

From the moment it is placed in New York Harbor, the Statue of Liberty becomes one of the nation's most important treasures. It will become more than a symbol of freedom. It will also become a symbol of welcome to millions of newcomers who see in America the chance to build better lives for themselves and their families.

The Statue of Liberty is there to greet them, but for the immigrants their ordeal in search of freedom and opportunity is far from over. As soon as their ship docks in the harbor, they line up at the rail, anxious to leave the vessel. There are millions of newcomers pouring in, however. The immigration depot cannot begin to process them all in a single day. After weeks at sea, many of the immigrants are forced to wait on board for as long as four more days.

ELLIS ISLAND

Between 1855 and 1890, the immigration depot where newcomers are processed is Castle Island, a huge round stone structure built in 1808 as a fort. It is here that more than eight million bewildered strangers will be introduced to America.

By 1890, Castle Island cannot handle the ever-increasing flood of arrivals. A new and much larger depot is built on New York Harbor's Ellis Island. Between 1892 and 1920, the busiest years of the facility, more than 23 million newcomers will enter America through Ellis Island. Even more than the Statue of Liberty, it will become the symbol of the immigrant experience.

Ellis Island—you got thousands of people marching in, a little bit excited, a little bit scared. Just imagine you're 14 ½ years old and you're in a strange country and you don't know what's going to happen.

—Albert Mardirossian,
Armenian immigrant

As the immigrants first set foot on American soil, their faces reveal the sense of anxiety shared by all strangers in a strange new land. Most cannot speak English and most have heard frightening stories of the ordeal that awaits them at Ellis Island.

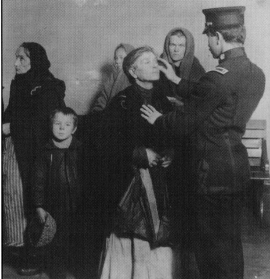

The immigrants' fears are justified. Once inside the Ellis Island facility, the newcomers are forced to wait hours, sometimes days, before undergoing both a physical and a verbal examination. They wait knowing that if they fail either test, they will be sent back across the ocean. The physical examination includes an eye test for trachoma, a disease common in southern and eastern Europe. About 2 percent of all the newcomers fail this or some other test and are forced to return to their homelands.

The verbal examinations are just as difficult, just as terrifying. Uniformed immigration officers, with the aid of interpreters, fire a battery of questions at the newcomers: "Where did you come from? Where are you headed? Can you read and write? Have you served time in prison? Do you have a job waiting for you?" Though most of the immigrants pass the test, it is a bewildering experience.

He asked me a lot of silly questions. You know what I mean? About America, if I knew all about America. Well, I didn't know anything about America.

—Florence Norris, English immigran

The Ellis Island experience is so bewildering that many immigrants actually lose their names in the process. Often, when the immigrants state their names, the officer writes down what he thinks he hears rather than what is said. When asked their names, many confused newcomers are apt to state the names of their hometowns or their former occupations instead. Some officers, on their own, change European-sounding names like "Valentin" to more American-sounding names like "William." Thousands enter America with their names changed forever.

Finally, for most, the Ellis Island ordeal is over. The immigrants gather on the docks awaiting the ferryboats that will take them across the harbor into New York. Many will journey on to other American cities like Boston, Philadelphia or Baltimore, but hundreds of thousands will make their new home in New York. As they gaze at the skyline of the world's largest city, they can only imagine what lies ahead.

THE TEEMING CITY

The immigrants who pour into American cities in the last decades of the 1800's arrive at a time of great change. The United States, long a country of farms and small towns, is increasingly becoming a nation of city dwellers. The cities offer goods and services that previous generations could never have imagined.

TO THE
VISITING
THOUSANDS

EXTENDS
THE KEY
TO THE
CITY

The cities are exciting, bustling places. They are filled with theaters and museums. They offer the latest in transportation. In every season of the year, they attract tens of thousands of pleasure seekers.

The city dazzled us. We had never seen such buildings, such people, such activity. Maybe the stories were true. Maybe everything was possible in America!

—Slovenian immigrant boy

The urban centers are continually growing. Enormous bridges joining various parts of the city are built across rivers bustling with a commerce of their own. When space becomes scarce, enterprising businesspeople erect buildings that rise upward, seeming to scrape the sky.

The city's department stores and specialty shops are filled with every type of product a person could want. Hundreds of elegant restaurants offer food from around the world. For those who can afford it, the city is truly a magical place.

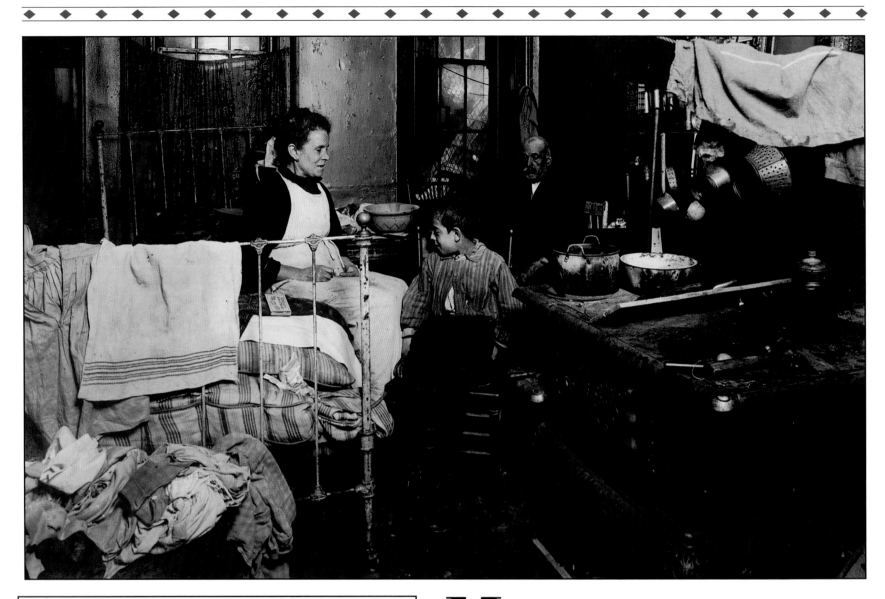

In America there were rooms without sunlight. . . . Where was there a place in America for me to play? . . . "Where is America?" cried my heart.

—Young immigrant girl

Most of the immigrants, however, are very poor. They have arrived in America with almost nothing. For them, the city is a very different kind of place. They cannot afford to shop in the stores or dine in the restaurants. They cannot even afford to live in clean, comfortable homes.

Most of the newcomers will be forced to live in dingy six- or seven-story buildings called tenements. They have been built by greedy landlords who know that most immigrants can afford nothing better. The tenements are horrible places, lacking clean air and light. Up to thirty-two families are crammed into each of these dwellings. Even the shortest tenement blocks house more than four thousand men, women and children.

For many new arrivals the tenements become their workplace as well as the place in which they live. Thousands cannot speak English, and until they learn this new language, their only way of making money is to take in work at home.

My uncles got jobs in a laundry uptown. My father wasn't so lucky. We took in work at home. But my father never lost hope. "We're in America," he'd say. "We'll work hard and things will get better." And he was right.
— Young Albanian immigrant

Whole families work long hours inside the tenements, sewing clothes, making paper flowers and sorting and labeling various types of goods. The pay for this piecework, as it is called, is very low, but the immigrants must do whatever it takes to survive in their new world.

THE CITY STREETS

For most of the immigrant city dwellers, the only escape from the dingy, overcrowded tenements is the street. There is sunlight in the streets, there is fresh air, and there are new arrivals from the Old World to meet and fellow immigrants with whom to share common experiences and news from back home.

RIVINGTON ST

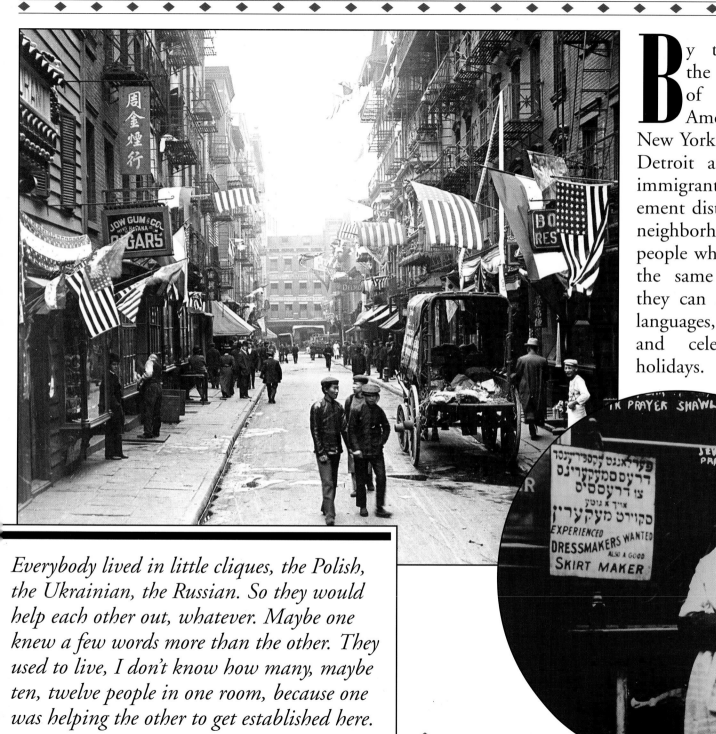

By the beginning of the 1900's, 75 percent of the residents of American cities like New York, Boston, Chicago, Detroit and Cleveland are immigrants. Within the tenement districts they settle in neighborhoods made up of people who have come from the same homeland. Here they can speak their native languages, buy familiar foods and celebrate traditional holidays.

Everybody lived in little cliques, the Polish, the Ukrainian, the Russian. So they would help each other out, whatever. Maybe one knew a few words more than the other. They used to live, I don't know how many, maybe ten, twelve people in one room, because one was helping the other to get established here.

—Louise Nagy, Polish immigrant

When I came to this country and I came to a pushcart on First Avenue, and I saw all those fruits and vegetables in February, that gave me such a lift. That I liked.

—Immigrant boy

Increasingly, with every passing year, the streets of many American cities take on the flavor of the Old World. They are filled with pushcarts from which enterprising immigrants, determined to escape tenement work, sell goods of all kinds.

For the immigrants, the streets become the very arteries of life. The newcomers have little money to travel far from their homes, but almost everything they can afford to buy can be found in their neighborhood streets.

Between the streets and the tenement buildings lie long, dark alleys. Like the tenements, they are unpleasant, dirty places. They are often the meeting spots of neighborhood gangs. Immigrant parents live in fear that their children will be influenced by those who have turned to crime out of frustration with the challenges of their life in the city.

Most immigrant children, however, avoid the gangs. There are no parks or other open spaces in their neighborhoods, so the streets become their playgrounds. They use their imaginations to create their own games and their own fun.

A GOOD EDUCATION

It is hard to be a stranger in a strange land. It is difficult and often frightening not knowing the language or the nation's ways. There is a way out, though. It is education. In school, the difficult English language can be learned. In school, children can begin to learn what it means to be an American.

Most immigrant parents understand that through schooling their children will have the opportunity to build better lives than they have had. As youngsters' education proceeds, an extraordinary thing takes place. Gradually, many of the children become wiser in the ways of America than their parents. In many immigrant homes, the children make decisions and take on tasks usually reserved for adult members of the family.

I was the one who always went to the gas company to complain about the bill. And I was the one who dealt with the landlords, the real estate agents. I could read the contract or the lease and speak English. I became in a sense a sort of junior father of the family.

—Immigrant boy

F or adults as well, education is the avenue to better jobs and a better life. It is also the road to one of their fondest dreams—that of becoming full-fledged American citizens.

My mother began to go to night school, and she immediately began to study for citizenship. She and I studied together about the Constitution, about the presidents, about the portions of the government, the executive, the judicial, and the congressional. She knew all these things and she did pass the examination and it was one of the happiest days of her life when she became a citizen.

—Morris Moel, Ukrainian
Jewish immigrant

פריע קלאסען אז ענגליש!

לערנט לעזען, שרײבען און רעדען
די שפּראך פון אײערע קינדער.

פארבערײטונג צו
ווערען א בירגער.
אלע סקול געגנ-
שטענדע. סמעציעלע
קלאסען פאר געביל-
דעטע אױסלענדער.

FREE CLASSES IN ENGLISH!

אינפארמאציע וועגען די קלאס-
ען קענט איהר קריגען אין...

LEARN TO SPEAK, READ
& WRITE THE LANGUAGE
OF YOUR CHILDREN.
NATURALIZATION PREP-
ARATION. ALL SCHOOL

**INFORMATION
& CLASSES AT.**

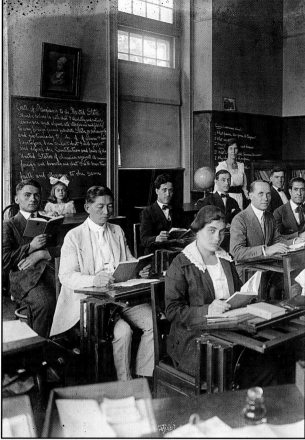

Millions of immigrant men and women attend classes especially created for them. They learn English, they study history and the laws of their new nation. Most attend their classes at night after completing a long day's work. They are determined not only to live in America but to become Americans as well.

HARD WORK

Education is a vital key to building one's future in America, but it does not take the immigrants long to discover that there is another key as well. In America, hard work can lead to success.

From the beginning, Americans have been a most industrious people. Hard work is a national characteristic. Throughout our history, artists, songwriters and journalists have found in the American worker a figure worthy of celebration.

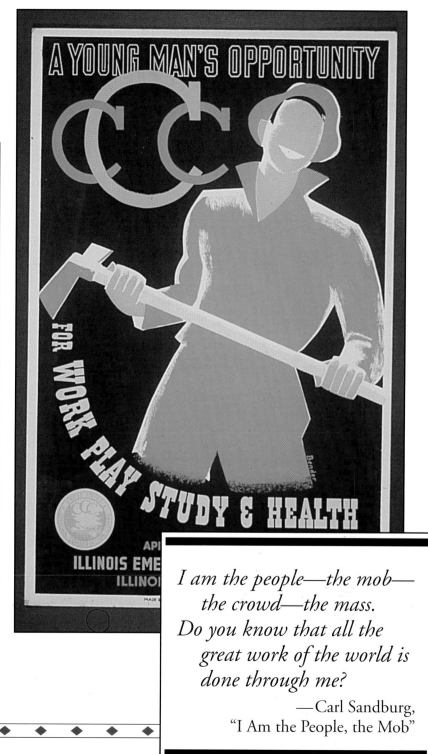

I am the people—the mob— the crowd—the mass. Do you know that all the great work of the world is done through me?

—Carl Sandburg,
"I Am the People, the Mob"

At first, it is not easy for most newcomers to find their way into the American work force. Many employers are put off by their accents and foreign ways. Native-born workers see them as a threat to their own jobs. In a nation caught up in enormous industrial growth, however, labor is greatly needed. Millions of new Americans find work in the nation's ever-increasing factories.

The factories become the workplace not only of the men but of tens of thousands of immigrant women as well. Factory pay is low, and most immigrant families need the wages of both husband and wife.

My mother was a twister in the Lawrence mills. It was unusual; in Italy there were no jobs for women. In fact, people that heard about it back in the village didn't like the idea of the women working. But my mother felt she was doing no different from all the other women, so she decided she was going to work. Make some money.

—Josephine Costanzo, Italian immigrant

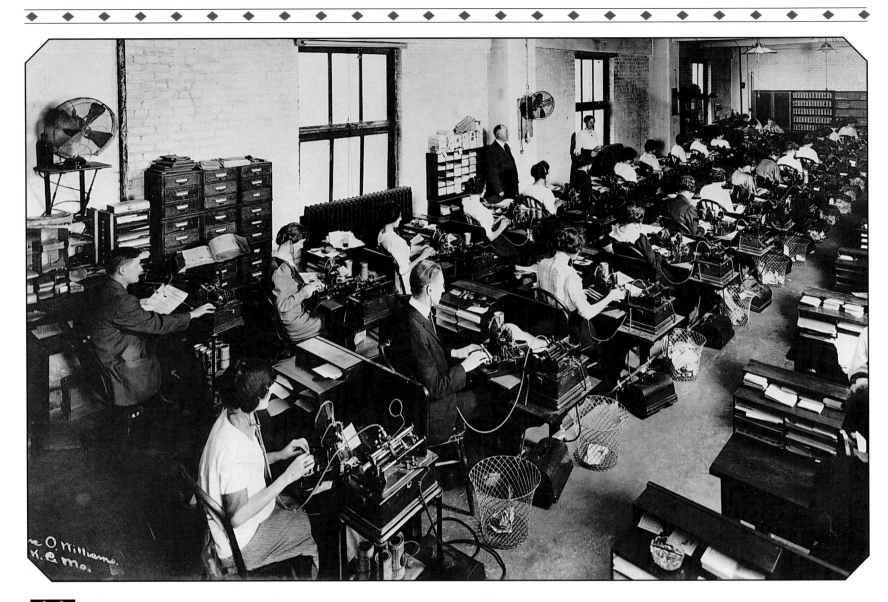

The O. Williams
K. C. mo.

Those who toil in the factories work long hours under difficult conditions, but soon there are other avenues of employment for women. As American factories and businesses continue to expand, the need to keep up with orders and other paperwork grows as well. Office workers are needed desperately. Thousands of immigrant women find work in these offices where they are surrounded by new inventions such as the typewriter, the dictating machine, the adding machine and the telephone.

The growth of the factories and offices leads to the continued growth of the cities. As more and more people pour in, new buildings, new trolley lines and new bridges must be erected to serve them. Immigrant laborers become an important part of the urban work force.

Building the cities is one thing; keeping them safe and clean is another. More and more police officers are needed to patrol the neighborhoods. Scores of other workers are needed to sweep the streets in summer and to keep them free of ice and snow in winter.

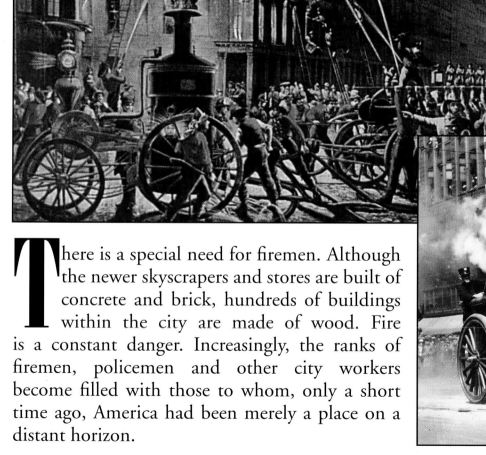

There is a special need for firemen. Although the newer skyscrapers and stores are built of concrete and brick, hundreds of buildings within the city are made of wood. Fire is a constant danger. Increasingly, the ranks of firemen, policemen and other city workers become filled with those to whom, only a short time ago, America had been merely a place on a distant horizon.

WORKING OUTSIDE THE CITY

UNITED MINE-WORKERS OF AMERICA.
UNITED WE STAND, DIVIDED WE FALL

The immigrants have arrived at a time of great growth outside the cities. The American continent is filled with natural resources. Many lie deep beneath the earth. Mining these resources is a terribly difficult and dangerous job, but thousands of immigrants, anxious to improve their lot, are willing to tackle it. Miles underground, they dig the coal, copper, zinc and other minerals that supply the fuel and raw materials for the ever-demanding American factories.

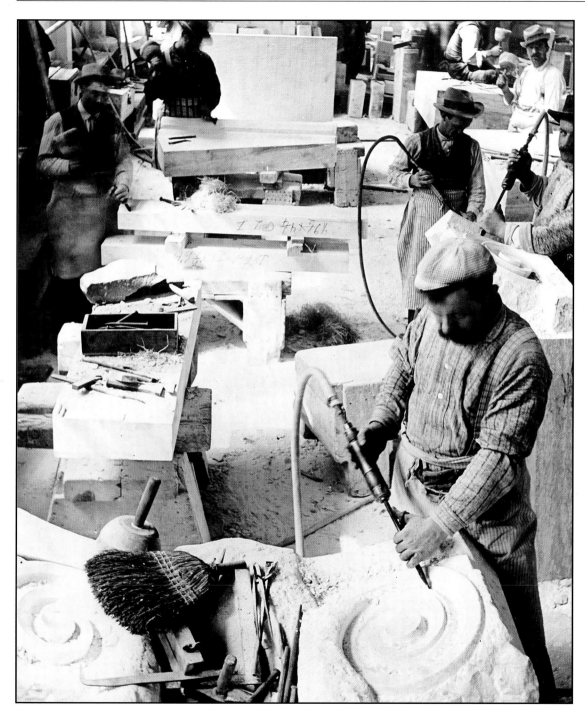

Above the earth, there are great resources as well. The nation's quarries yield enormous amounts of marble and other stone. Many immigrants are employed in mining this resource. Others, trained in Old World countries, use their skills to create magnificent stone carvings that will adorn buildings throughout the nation.

There is another great resource that lies above the ground. America is a land of vast, magnificent forests. Billions of trees yield the lumber from which homes, offices and other buildings are erected. Into the great forests of the midwestern and far northwestern states come lumberjacks, who chop down the trees and haul them off to the sawmills. Many immigrant men find their first jobs in America surrounded by the tallest living things on earth.

Tens of thousands of other immigrants find work in the nation's steel mills. By 1900, America has become the industrial leader of the world, and by 1910, over half of America's industrial workers are immigrants.

Where would your mines have been dug and worked, where would your great iron industries and constructions . . . have been were it not for the immigrants? . . . It is the immigrant that bears the burden of hard labor . . . and has contributed his full share to the building up of our great country.

—Representative Samuel McMillan of New York, speech to Congress, 1908

The biggest employer of all, by far, is the American railroad system. By the 1870's, great railroad lines run three thousand miles from coast to coast. The earliest of these transcontinental systems have been built largely through the efforts of Chinese and Irish laborers. Millions of other immigrants find work on the railroad. They lay the tracks, keep them open, repair the engines and work in the depots and on the trains.

All those bridges, all those roads, all those railroads—they were built by people who worked hard.

—Joseph Baccardo, Italian immigrant

The railroad becomes the symbol of might and progress, and the immigrants become the symbol of all that can be accomplished in America. Through education and hard work, millions have established themselves in a new world. In the process, they have helped build a nation.

PIONEERS!

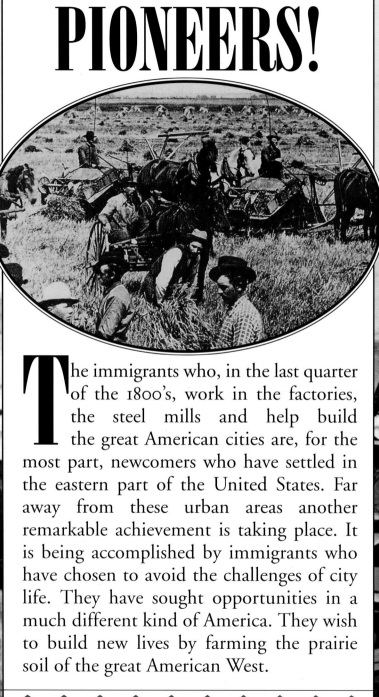

The immigrants who, in the last quarter of the 1800's, work in the factories, the steel mills and help build the great American cities are, for the most part, newcomers who have settled in the eastern part of the United States. Far away from these urban areas another remarkable achievement is taking place. It is being accomplished by immigrants who have chosen to avoid the challenges of city life. They have sought opportunities in a much different kind of America. They wish to build new lives by farming the prairie soil of the great American West.

In the last decades of the 1800's, the vast territories of the American West are being settled by millions of courageous men, women and children. The earliest of these pioneers have made the long, dangerous journey across the continent on foot, in covered wagons, and by stagecoach and steamboat. Now the expanding railroad system, which is being built with the aid of immigrant labor, is bringing millions of others to the western lands.

Only an emigrant! son of the soil,
With my hands ready for labor and toil,
Willing for anything honest I be,
Surely there's room on the prairies for me;
— From song, "Only an Emigrant"

For the countless immigrants who want to avoid the crowded cities, the western territories offer the best hope for a new and better life in their new country. Those who can afford it head west by train immediately upon entering America. Others live in the city long enough to earn the train fare and then head west. Increasingly, the connecting western railroad depots take on the look of Ellis Island.

Many of the immigrants come from the Scandinavian countries of Sweden, Denmark, Finland and Norway. Most were farmers in their native lands. No matter how poor they were, they were surrounded by clean air and sunshine. There is plenty of fresh air and sunshine on the western prairies, and there is the opportunity to own their own land. The United States government has provided that 160 acres, or one quarter of a square mile, will be given to any head of a family who will live on the land and farm it for at least five years.

There is opportunity, but there are many hardships as well. Almost no trees grow on the prairie, and the settlers must live in houses made of prairie sod. Often there is too much sunshine. Long periods without rain dry up the land and cause prairie fires and fierce dust storms. In the winter, blizzards cover the prairie with mountains of snow. The greatest hardship of all, though, is loneliness. Unlike the immigrants in the city, who face the challenges of terrible overcrowding, the immigrants who choose to settle in the West must deal with a life in which the nearest neighbor may be thirty or forty miles away.

Using the labor of every member of the family, the immigrant pioneers break the rich prairie soil and plant their crops. They will work every day from sunup to sundown, with little time for rest or recreation. Like the immigrants in the city, those who have chosen to face the challenges of the West are determined to succeed.

Those who survive their earliest hardships are aided greatly by the spirit of inventiveness that sweeps America in the last decades of the 1800's. Every week seems to bring new inventions and new machines. Many of the new machines are designed to make farming more productive. By the late 1870's, farm machinery of every kind dominates the western landscape. More crops than could ever have been imagined can be planted and harvested in less time and with fewer hands than ever before.

By the 1890's, the once empty prairies of the American West are covered with crops. The western immigrants and their fellow pioneers are feeding the nation and much of the rest of the world. Like their fellow immigrants in the East, they too have helped build America.

No wonder that so many Europeans who have never been able to say that such a portion of land was theirs, cross the Atlantic to realize that happiness.

—Alexis de Tocqueville,
early French traveler in America

TODAY'S IMMIGRANTS

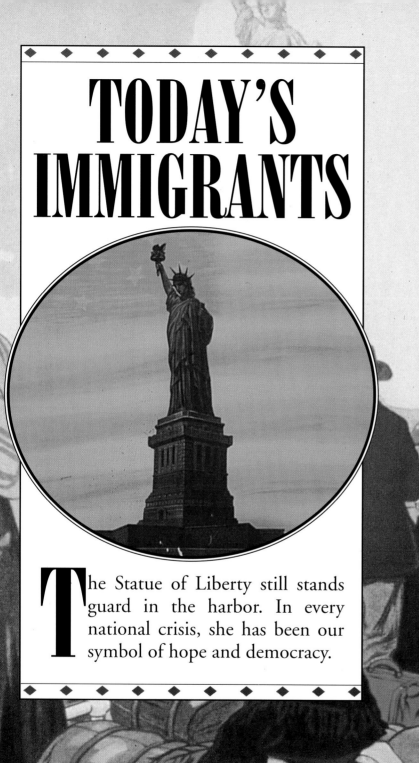

The Statue of Liberty still stands guard in the harbor. In every national crisis, she has been our symbol of hope and democracy.

Immigrants from around the world still look to America as the land of freedom and opportunity. Most modern newcomers come from countries different from those of the earlier arrivals. Many come from nations throughout Asia, Africa, the Caribbean, or from various Spanish-speaking countries. Like those who came before them, most will meet the challenges of life in a new land and will realize their dream of becoming citizens of America.

Of course, there's many things I miss about my homeland. It's a beautiful country. But I just couldn't earn a living there. So far it's not been easy here in America either. But my kids are getting a better education. And we have more freedom than we've ever had.

—George Hamayaz, Venezuelan immigrant

Today, four out of every ten Americans are descended from ancestors who passed through Ellis Island. Most are keenly aware of those who were willing to make many sacrifices so that future generations might prosper.

My parents and my grandparents were all born in the old country. They came to America for our sake. It was their greatest gift to us.

—Samuel Villani, son of Italian parents

Tens of thousands of the most recent immigrants come from African nations. Here, they join tens of millions of African Americans whose ancestors were brought to the United States in chains. Slavery represents this country's most horrible and most inexcusable experience. Yet millions of African Americans have overcome the greatest obstacles of all and have made vital contributions in every area of our society. Like others whose roots lie in countries around the world, they proudly contribute their traditions, beliefs, foods, customs and culture to the mosaic that is America.

The American culture is the culture of many lands. What we eat, how we talk, the way we dress and what we believe are the result of the contributions of people from every corner of the globe. We borrow from every group and are made richer by the borrowing.

On special days I get to dress as my great-grandparents did. It's fun. I'm proud to be an American, but I'm proud of my roots too.

—Girl of Polish ancestry

W e are a nation of immigrants. Our forefathers and foremothers have left us their spirit, their cultures and their dreams.

Our cultural diversity is our greatest strength, for we are more than a nation. Thanks to those who dared to be immigrants, we are a nation of nations. It is a heritage of which we should all be proud.

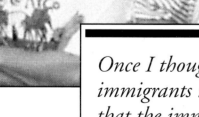

Once I thought to write the story of the immigrants in America. Then I realized that the immigrants were America's story.

—Oscar Handlin, American historian

The Library of Congress

All of the photographs, lithographs, engravings, paintings, line drawings, posters, song lyrics, song-sheet covers, broadsides and other illustrative materials contained in this book have been culled from the collections of the Library of Congress. The Library houses the largest collection of stored knowledge on earth. Within its walls lie treasures that show us how much more than a "library" a great library can be.

The statistics that help define the Library are truly amazing. It has more books from America and England than anywhere else, yet barely one half of its collections are in English. It contains more maps, globes, charts and atlases than any other place on earth. It houses one of the largest collections of photographs in the world, the largest collection of films in America, almost every phonograph record ever made in the United States and the collections of the American Folklife Center. The Library also contains over six million volumes on hard sciences and applied technology.

It is a very modern institution as well. Dr. James Billington, the Librarian of Congress, has defined the Library's future through his vision of a "library without walls." "I see the Library of Congress in the future," he has said, "as an active catalyst for civilization, not just a passive mausoleum of cultural accomplishments of the past."

The Library of Congress was originally established to serve the members of Congress. Over the years it has evolved into a great national library. Unlike almost every other national library in the world, the Library of Congress does not limit the use of its collections to accredited scholars. Ours is a national library made by the people for the people, and is open to all the people. Fondly referred to as "the storehouse of the national memory," it is truly one of our proudest and most important possessions.

Index

Numbers in *italics* indicate photographs, illustrations and charts.